D0518928

HAPPINESS

THOUGHTS AND QUOTATIONS FOR EVERY DAY

summersdale

HAPPINESS

An Hachette UK Company
www.hachette.co.uk

Summersdale Publishers Ltd
Part of Octopus Publishing Group Limited
Carmelite House
50 Victoria Embankment
LONDON
EC4Y 0DZ
UK

www.summersdale.com

Printed and bound in the Czech Republic

ISBN: 978-1-78685-243-4

Substantial discounts on bulk quantities of Summersdale books are available to corporations, professional associations and other organisations. For details contact general enquiries: telephone: +44 (0) 1243 771107 or email: enquiries@summersdale.com.

To ....

From ....

Happiness is when
what you think, what
you say and what you
do are in harmony.

Mahatma Gandhi

One joy scatters
a hundred griefs.

Chinese proverb

Happiness makes up
in height for what it
lacks in length.

Robert Frost

He who sows courtesy reaps friendship, and he who plants kindness gathers love.

St Basil of Caesarea

HAPPINESS IS NOT SOMETHING READY-MADE. IT COMES FROM YOUR OWN ACTIONS.

Dalai Lama

The best way to cheer yourself up is to try to cheer somebody else up.

Mark Twain

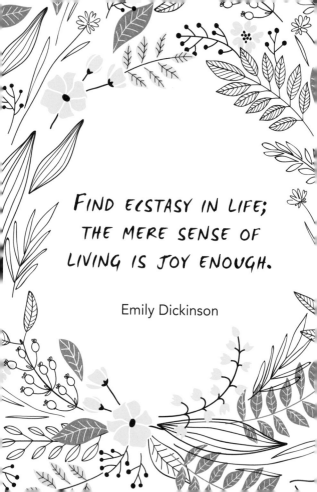

FIND ECSTASY IN LIFE;
THE MERE SENSE OF
LIVING IS JOY ENOUGH.

Emily Dickinson

Happiness CONSISTS *not in having much, but in being* CONTENT *with little.*

Marguerite Gardiner

HAPPINESS IS NOT AN IDEAL OF REASON, BUT OF IMAGINATION.

Immanuel Kant

Have patience
and endure: this
unhappiness will one
day be beneficial.

Ovid

I began learning long ago that those who are happiest are those who do the most for others.

Booker T. Washington

MINDFULNESS HELPS
US TO REGAIN THE
PARADISE WE THOUGHT
WE HAD LOST.

Thích Nhất Hạnh

Success is not the key to

HAPPINESS.

Happiness is the key to

SUCCESS.

Albert Schweitzer

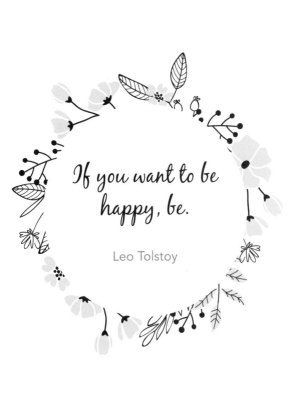

If you want to be happy, be.

Leo Tolstoy

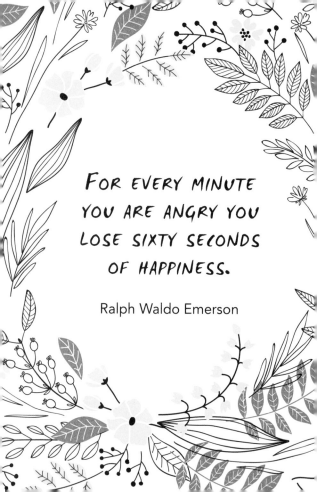

FOR EVERY MINUTE
YOU ARE ANGRY YOU
LOSE SIXTY SECONDS
OF HAPPINESS.

Ralph Waldo Emerson

THE
RIGHTEOUS
MAN IS
HAPPY IN
THIS WORLD,
AND HE IS
HAPPY IN
THE NEXT.

The Dhammapada

TURN YOUR FACE TO THE SUN AND THE SHADOWS FALL BEHIND YOU.

Maori proverb

HUMOUR

is the great thing, the

SAVING

thing.

Mark Twain

HAPPINESS BELONGS TO THE SELF-SUFFICIENT.

Aristotle

OUR LIFE IS WHAT
OUR THOUGHTS
MAKE IT.

Marcus Aurelius

HE WHO
KNOWS THAT
ENOUGH IS
ENOUGH WILL
ALWAYS HAVE
ENOUGH.

Lao Tzu

You will never
be happier
THAN YOU EXPECT.
To change your
happiness, change
YOUR EXPECTATION.

Bette Davis

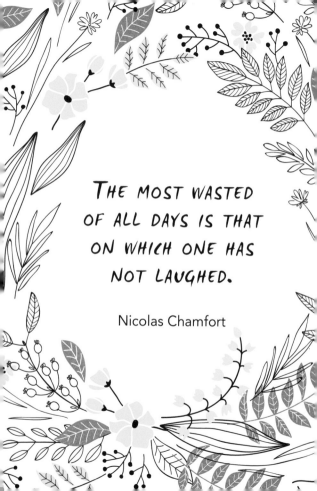

THE MOST WASTED
OF ALL DAYS IS THAT
ON WHICH ONE HAS
NOT LAUGHED.

Nicolas Chamfort

A GREAT
OBSTACLE TO
HAPPINESS
IS TO EXPECT
TOO MUCH
HAPPINESS.

Bernard de Fontenelle

Weeping may endure for a night, but joy comes in the morning.

Psalms 30:5

RULES FOR HAPPINESS:

*something to do,
someone to love,
something to hope for.*

Immanuel Kant

MOST FOLKS ARE ABOUT
AS HAPPY AS THEY MAKE
UP THEIR MINDS TO BE.

Abraham Lincoln

Happiness
never decreases by
being shared.

Buddha

The best way
to secure future
happiness is to
be as happy as
is rightfully
possible today.

Charles W. Eliot

THERE ARE TWO
WAYS OF SPREADING
LIGHT: TO BE THE
CANDLE OR THE
MIRROR THAT
REFLECTS IT.

Edith Wharton

The happiness of
your life depends
on the quality of
your thoughts.

Marcus Aurelius

IF YOU WANT
TO LIVE A
HAPPY LIFE,
TIE IT TO A
GOAL, NOT
TO PEOPLE
OR THINGS.

Albert Einstein

Seek to do good, and you will find that happiness will run after you.

James Freeman Clarke

HAPPINESS... LIES IN THE JOY OF ACHIEVEMENT, IN THE THRILL OF CREATIVE EFFORT.

Franklin D. Roosevelt

Happiness is a
habit – cultivate it.

Elbert Hubbard

Those who bring
sunshine into the
lives of others
cannot keep it
from themselves.

J. M. Barrie

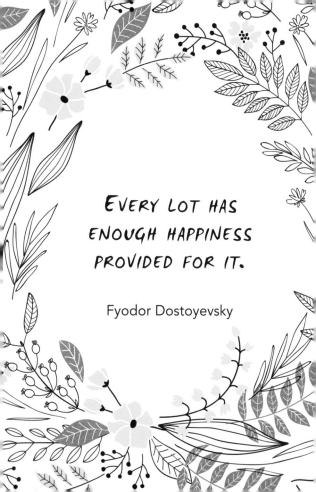

EVERY LOT HAS
ENOUGH HAPPINESS
PROVIDED FOR IT.

Fyodor Dostoyevsky

HAPPINESS
IS NOT A
GOAL; IT IS A
BY-PRODUCT
OF A LIFE
WELL LIVED.

Eleanor Roosevelt

Happiness is like a butterfly which, when pursued, is always beyond our grasp, but, if you will sit down quietly, may alight upon you.

Nathaniel Hawthorne

SO LONG
AS WE CAN
LOSE ANY
HAPPINESS,
WE POSSESS
SOME.

Booth Tarkington

A HANDFUL
OF HAPPINESS
IS BETTER THAN
A LOAF FULL
OF WISDOM.

Russian proverb

All that we need to
make us really happy
is something to be
enthusiastic about.

Charles Kingsley

A happy life consists not in the absence, but in the mastery of hardships.

Helen Keller

ALL THE
STATISTICS
IN THE
WORLD CAN'T
MEASURE THE
WARMTH OF
A SMILE.

Chris Hart

ILLUSORY
JOY IS OFTEN
WORTH MORE
THAN GENUINE
SORROW.

René Descartes

ALWAYS LAUGH WHEN
YOU CAN. IT IS
CHEAP MEDICINE.

Lord Byron

If you ever find
happiness by hunting
for it, you will
find it, as the old
woman did her lost
spectacles, safe on
her own nose all
the time.

Josh Billings

To be kind to all, to like many and love a few… is certainly the nearest we can come to happiness.

Mary Stuart

Mix a little FOOLISHNESS *with your serious plans. It is* LOVELY TO BE SILLY *at the right moment.*

Horace

Independence is happiness.

Susan B. Anthony

A happy life
consists in tranquillity
of mind.

Marcus Tullius Cicero

WHAT SUNSHINE IS TO FLOWERS, SMILES ARE TO HUMANITY.

Joseph Addison

The robbed
that smiles,

STEALS

SOMETHING

from the thief,

William Shakespeare

HE WHO ENJOYS DOING
AND ENJOYS WHAT HE
HAS DONE IS HAPPY.

Johann Wolfgang von Goethe

Happiness arises
in a state of peace,
not of tumult.

Ann Radcliffe

Grief can take
care of itself, but
to get the full value
of a joy you must
have somebody to
divide it with.

Mark Twain

Content makes
poor men rich;
discontent makes
rich men poor.

Benjamin Franklin

IF I
KEEP A GREEN
BOUGH IN MY
HEART THE
SINGING BIRD
WILL COME.

Chinese proverb

IF YOU MAKE UP YOUR MIND NOT TO BE HAPPY THERE'S NO REASON WHY YOU SHOULDN'T HAVE A FAIRLY GOOD TIME.

Edith Wharton

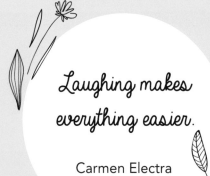

Laughing makes everything easier.

Carmen Electra

A kind heart is a
fountain of gladness,
making everything in
its vicinity freshen
into smiles.

Washington Irving

HAPPINESS OFTEN SNEAKS IN THROUGH A DOOR YOU DIDN'T KNOW YOU LEFT OPEN.

John Barrymore

THINK OF ALL
THE BEAUTY
STILL LEFT
AROUND
YOU AND
BE HAPPY.

Anne Frank

Forget not that the
earth delights to
feel your bare feet
and the winds long to
play with your hair.

Kahlil Gibran

Be glad of life
because it gives you
the chance to love,
to work, to play
and to look up
at the stars.

Henry van Dyke

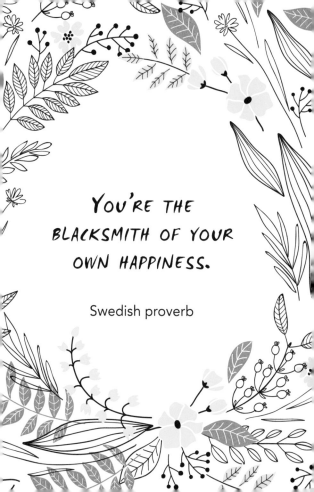

You're the Blacksmith of Your Own Happiness.

Swedish proverb

The right to happiness is fundamental.

Anna Pavlova

Joy is of the will
WHICH LABOURS,
which overcomes
OBSTACLES,
which
KNOWS TRIUMPH.

William Butler Yeats

IT IS NOT
HOW MUCH
WE HAVE, BUT
HOW MUCH
WE ENJOY,
THAT MAKES
HAPPINESS.

Charles Spurgeon

Pleasure in the
task puts perfection
in the work.

Aristotle

Wear a smile and have friends; wear a scowl and have wrinkles.

George Eliot

THOSE WHO MAKE
MANY FRIENDS... MAKE
SOCIETY A BETTER
PLACE AND LEAD HAPPY,
SATISFYING LIVES.

Daisaku Ikeda

Be happy. It's one way of being wise.

Colette

Action may not always bring happiness, but there is no happiness without action.

Benjamin Disraeli

Every day, tell at least one person something you like, admire or appreciate about them.

Richard Carlson

But what is happiness
except the simple
harmony between
a man and the life
he leads?

Albert Camus

THE TRUE
WAY TO
RENDER
OURSELVES
HAPPY IS
TO LOVE
OUR WORK
AND FIND
IN IT OUR
PLEASURE.

Françoise Bertaut de Motteville

GREATER HAPPINESS
COMES WITH SIMPLICITY
THAN WITH COMPLEXITY.

Buddha

Let us be
of good cheer,
remembering that the
misfortunes hardest
to bear are those
which never come.

James Russell Lowell

One must never
look for happiness:
one meets it
by the way.

Isabelle Eberhardt

If you want others
to be happy, practise
compassion. If you
want to be happy,
practise compassion.

Dalai Lama

THERE IS NO DUTY WE SO MUCH UNDERRATE AS THE DUTY OF BEING HAPPY.

Robert Louis Stevenson

THERE IS ONLY ONE HAPPINESS IN LIFE, TO LOVE AND BE LOVED.

George Sand

LAUGHTER IS THE
SENSATION OF
FEELING GOOD ALL
OVER AND SHOWING
IT PRINCIPALLY
IN ONE PLACE.

Josh Billings

Pleasure
disappoints,
possibility never.

Søren Kierkegaard

Happiness is the meaning and the purpose of life, the whole aim and end of human existence.

Aristotle

THERE ARE
THOSE WHO
GIVE WITH
JOY, AND
THAT JOY
IS THEIR
REWARD.

Kahlil Gibran

AGAINST THE
ASSAULT OF LAUGHTER
NOTHING CAN STAND.

Mark Twain

ALL ANIMALS,
EXCEPT MAN, KNOW
THAT THE PRINCIPAL
BUSINESS OF LIFE
IS TO ENJOY IT.

Samuel Butler

HAPPINESS CANNOT COME FROM WITHOUT. IT MUST COME FROM WITHIN.

Helen Keller

Happiness is a
perfume you cannot
pour on others
without getting
a few drops on
yourself.

 Ralph Waldo Emerson

WISDOM IS THE
SUPREME PART
OF HAPPINESS.

Sophocles

If you're interested in finding out more about our books, find us on Facebook at Summersdale Publishers and follow us on Twitter at @Summersdale.

www.summersdale.com